# TOP TEN
# SLOWEST

Ruth Owen

*Saguaro cacti, USA*

Publisher: Melissa Fairley
Art Director: Faith Booker
Editor: Emma Dods
Designer: Emma Randall
Production Controller: Ed Green
Production Manager: Suzy Kelly

ISBN: 978 1 84898 207 9

Copyright © *TickTock* Entertainment Ltd. 2010
First published in Great Britain in 2010 by *TickTock* Entertainment Ltd.,
The Old Sawmill, 103 Goods Station Road, Tunbridge Wells, Kent, TN1 2DP

Printed in China
1 3 5 7 9 10 8 6 4 2

A CIP catalogue record for this book is available from the British Library.
All rights reserved. No part of this publication may be reproduced, copied, stored in a retrieval
system or transmitted in any form or by any means electronic, mechanical, photocopying,
recording or otherwise without prior written permission of the copyright owner.

Picture credits (t=top; b=bottom; c=centre; l=left; r=right; OFC=outside front cover):
Aflo Co. Ltd./Alamy: 5t, 18–19, 28b. iStock: 1, 4, 10–11, 14–15, 29tr. Jan-Pieter Fuhr: 24, 25t, 25b, 29br.
William Leaman/Alamy: 11c. NASA/courtesy of nasaimages.org: 21b, 29cl. NASA Kennedy Space Center/
courtesy of nasaimages.org: 20–21. Carla Thomas, NASA/courtesy of nasaimages.org: OFC, 2, 12–13,
29tl. Courtesy of ThyssenKrupp Fördertechnik: 5b, 22–23, 29bl. Courtesy of Mark Scase: 6–7, 28cl.
Denis Scott/Corbis: 16–17, 28cr. Shutterstock: 26. Roy Toft/Getty Images: 8–9, 28tl. Jim Zipp/Ardea: 27.

### Thank you to Lorraine Petersen and the members of nasen

Every effort has been made to trace copyright holders, and we apologize in advance for any omissions.
We would be pleased to insert the appropriate acknowledgements in any subsequent edition of this publication.

NOTE TO READERS
The website addresses are correct at the time of publishing. However, due to the ever-changing
nature of the internet, websites and content may change. Some websites can contain links that
are unsuitable for children. The publisher is not responsible for changes in content or website
addresses. We advise that internet searches should be supervised by an adult.

# CONTENTS

*Helios, an unmanned plane*

# INTRODUCTION

**This book is all about the world's slowest things.**

From slow animals…

…to slow journeys…

…to **SLOW** machines.

Sloths are so slow that algae grows on them. This makes them look green.

To experience the slowest express train, jump aboard the Glacier Express in Switzerland.

The giant *Bagger 288* has a top speed of just 0.6 kilometres per hour.

# SLOWEST RACE

**The slowest race in the world is the World Snail Racing Championship.**

Since 1970, the championship has been held every year in the UK. The track is 33 centimetres of wet table.

The fastest ever winner was named Archie.
Archie reached the finish line in two minutes.
Some snails are so slow they never make
it to the end!

# SLOWEST MAMMAL

**The world's slowest mammal is the three-toed sloth.**

Sloths live in rainforests in Central and South America.

Sloths hang upside down in the trees. They move very, very, slowly. Their average speed is 0.24 kilometres per hour.

They sleep, eat and even give birth hanging in trees.

To go to the toilet, sloths need to climb down to the ground. Luckily they only need to go to the toilet once a week!

# SLOWEST GROWING

**The saguaro cactus is one of the world's slowest growing plants. It grows in the Sonoran Desert in the USA.**

The saguaro grows to around 12 metres tall.
It can take 150 years to reach this height.

It can take up to 10 years to grow
a couple of centimetres!

Birds help the saguaro to spread its seeds.
The saguaro produces juicy, red fruit.
Birds eat the seeds then spread them
around in their poo!

*A Curved-bill thrasher bird
eating saguaro cactus fruit.*

# SLOWEST PLANE

**Helios was probably the slowest plane ever, reaching a top speed of 37 kilometres per hour. A person riding a bicycle could overtake it.**

*Solar cells*

Helios was an unmanned experimental plane. It was built by scientists at NASA. Unfortunately Helios crashed in 2003.

*Propeller*

Helios used solar energy to power its propellers.
Solar cells collected the Sun's energy.

# SLOWEST BUILD

**In Spain, there is a church named La Sagrada Família. The building of the church began in 1882. It is still going on today!**

Why is it taking so long to build the church? Lack of money is one reason. The building work is paid for by donations. Donations are gifts of money. In 1936 parts of the church were destroyed in the Spanish Civil War. They have had to be rebuilt.

Building work has never stopped though! The church should be finished by 2025.

Although this is slow, building work has taken longer.
The Great Wall of China took over 2,000 years to build!

# SLOWEST HEARTBEAT

**The mammal with the slowest heartbeat is believed to be the blue whale.**

The heartbeat of a blue whale is between 4–8 beats per minute.

The average resting human heartbeat is around 70 beats per minute.

A whale's heart can weigh around one tonne – that's as much as a small car!

# SLOWEST TRAIN

**The Glacier Express is known as "the slowest express train in the world". It travels at 30 kilometres per hour.**

The Glacier Express is in Switzerland. It travels between the towns of St Moritz and Zermatt. The train takes 7.5 hours to travel 291 kilometres.

The ride takes you over 291 bridges and through 91 tunnels.

# SLOWEST VEHICLE

The Crawler-Transporter is a giant tracked vehicle. It weighs 2,721 tonnes.

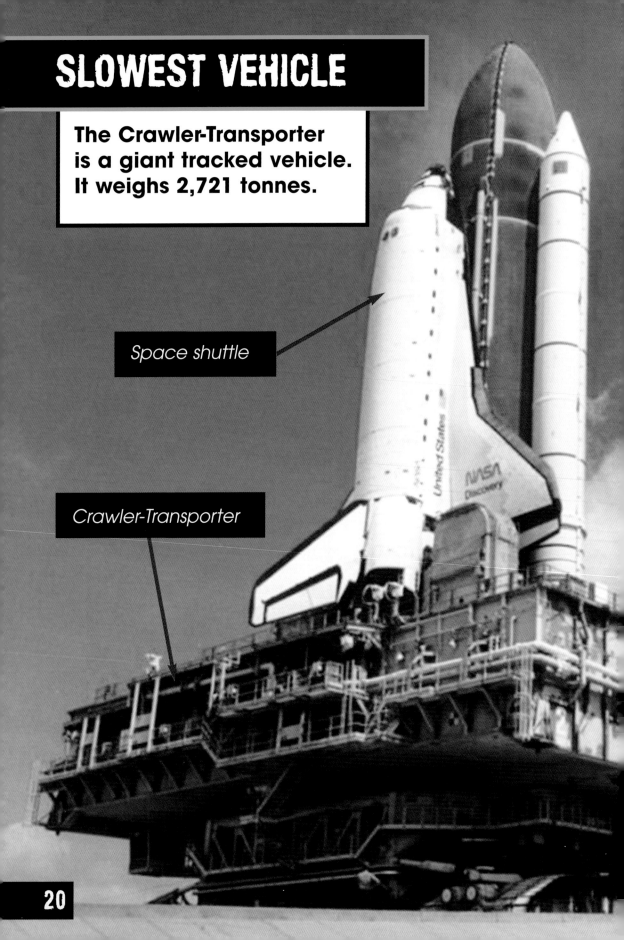

Space shuttle

Crawler-Transporter

There are two Crawler-Transporters at the Kennedy Space Center in Florida, USA.

They transport the space shuttle from the vehicle assembly building to the launch pad.

The Crawler-Transporter moves at just 1.6 kilometres per hour when it is loaded!

Tracks

# SLOWEST MOVING MACHINE

The *Bagger 288* is one of the world's largest digging machines. It is used in open coal mines in Germany.

The *Bagger 288* is 240 metres long and 96 metres high. When the machine has to travel, it is very slow. Its top speed is 0.6 kilometres per hour.

Bagger 288

In 2001, the machine had to move from one coal mine to another. It had to cross many roads, a river and a railway line. It took three weeks for the machine to travel just 22 kilometres.

# SLOWEST MUSIC

**The world's longest, slowest piece of music is being played in a church in Germany.**

The music was written by an American composer named John Cage. He called the music "As Slow As Possible".

A group of musicians are making the piece of music last for 639 years!

*St Burchadi Church in Halberstadt, Germany*

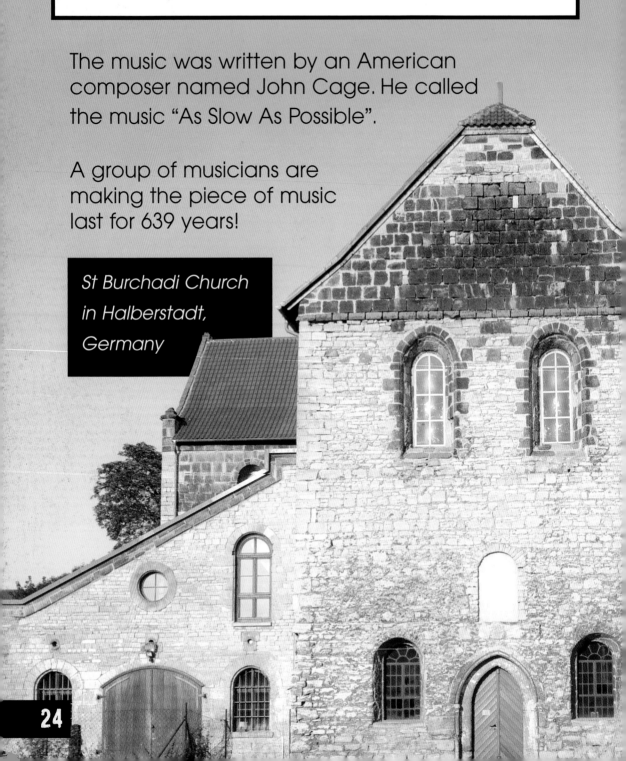

The piece of music began in 2001. It is being played on an organ. Each chord or note lasts for months at a time.

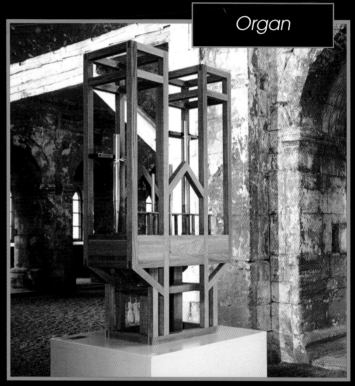

*Organ*

To keep the note playing for months, weights are put on the organ pedals. The final note will be played sometime in the year 2640.

*Weights on pedals*

# SLOW ANIMALS

## In the sea

Seahorses are the slowest fish in the world. Their average speed is about 0.016 kilometres per hour.

The world's fastest fish is the sailfish. Sailfish can swim at 110 kilometres per hour over short distances.

## In the air

The slowest flying bird is the American woodcock. It flies at just 8 kilometres per hour.

The fastest flying bird is the grey-headed albatross. One bird was measured flying 127 kilometres per hour.

# TOP TEN SLOWEST

**Nature sometimes takes it really slow.**

*Three-toed sloth*

*Saguaro cactus*

*Snail*

*Blue whale*

**Sometimes the journey is more important than the destination.**

*Glacier Express*

**Some man-made things are slow but useful.**

*Helios*

*Crawler-Transporter*

Bagger 288

**Some things are slow but worth waiting for.**

*La Sagrada Família*

**And some slow things are strange but true!**

*"As Slow As Possible"*

# NEED TO KNOW WORDS

**algae** Water plants that do not have leaves, roots or stems.

**composer** A person who writes music.

**donation** Something that is given as a gift, e.g. money.

**experimental** Something that is part of an experiment, or something that is being tried out or tested.

**express** A service which is faster than usual.

**mammal** An animal with fur or hair that gives birth to a live baby and feeds it with milk from its own body. A mammal's body temperature stays the same no matter how hot or cold the air or water is around it.

**NASA** This stands for National Aeronautics and Space Administration. NASA is an organization of the American government that runs America's space programme.

**open coal mine** A mine where coal is dug from the ground on the Earth's surface, instead of underground.

**propeller** Two or more blades which turn at high speed and make a ship or aircraft move.

**solar energy** Light or heat that comes from the Sun.

**Spanish Civil War** A conflict in Spain that took place between 1936 and 1939.

**Unmanned** Without a crew.

# SLOW FACTS

- Venus is the slowest spinning planet in our solar system. The Earth spins around once in 24 hours. It takes Venus 243 Earth days to spin around once!

- One type of deep-sea clam grows very slowly. It takes 100 years to reach one centimetre in length.

# FIND OUT MORE ONLINE...

Guinness World Records
http://www.guinnessworldrecords.com

La Sagrada Famíla
http://www.sagradafamilia.cat/

National Geographic
http://animals.nationalgeographic.com/
animals/a-to-z

Snail Racing Championships
http://www.scase.co.uk/snailracing/

# INDEX